eating to

CON

PAGE

Welcome to the first-ever Irish rugby players' cookbook! From the beginning, our challenge has been to create not just another cookbook, but something that marries the essence of the players' and their favourite dishes. In short, a cookbook that is highly informative, easy to use and fun to read. Whether you're a rugby fan, cooking enthusiast or are just curious about your favourite player's party piece, there's something here for everyone!

Most of Ireland's leading rugby players' have given us their favourite recipes for what they eat when preparing for big matches, as well as what they eat post-match or relaxing at home. All meals can be cooked for friends and family and contain nutritional values such as fat, calories and carbohydrates. A general nutrition section is also included to give readers advice on maintaining an active lifestyle. Useful, practical tips on training for a sports event are provided for those who are more athletic in nature, as well as the healthy habits of successful athletes.

All proceeds from the sales of this cookbook are going towards the IRUPA Injured Players' Fund. While the rewards of playing top-level rugby are extremely attractive, the precariousness of a career in rugby is a continuous reminder of just how fortunate most players' are. The fund reflects the players' commitment towards supporting those players' who have had to depart from rugby or may have to in the near future due to a life-threatening or paralysis injury or illness.

A lot of people have helped to make the book a reality. I'd like to thank all those companies who generously supported the book through advertising; without this assistance the whole concept would not have been possible.

Gina, John & Tara at Zahra Publishing, who right from our first meeting were so enthusiastic about the book and are largely responsible for the book being so professional and entertaining. Thanks also to Sarah Keogh who provided all the nutritional information.

To Lorna in our offices who undertook the huge task of having to acquire all the required information from the players'. Finally I'd like to thank all the players' themselves for giving their time and support to such a worthy cause. I hope you enjoy the book!

Happy eating,

Niall Woods
CEO
IRUPA (Irish Rugby Union Players' Association)

Nutrition for Fitness

Whether you are a professional athlete or an amateur enthusiast, what you eat and how you eat can have a huge impact on how well you train and how well you perform when you exercise. Getting the most out of any sport requires dedication and regular training, and one important part of training is making sure you are getting all the nutrients you need, in the right amounts.

While eating well won't turn you into a superstar, there are many ways that good nutrition can help maximise the skills and abilities you already have – and ignoring nutrition can stop you from reaching your full potential.

Bread – all kinds
Breakfast cereals
Potatoes
Pasta
Rice
Noodles
Pulses – beans,
lentils and peas
Fruit – fresh, tinned,
frozen and dried
Root vegetables –
carrots, parsnip and
turnip

TIP - you need less energy
when you are not training or
exercising. To avoid gaining
weight out of season,
remember to reduce the
amount of food and snacks you
eat if you don't exercise at
certain times of the year.

**SUGARY
FOODS**

Jams and
marmalades
Sugar
Fruit cakes – brack,
fruit scones
Desserts such as
fruit crumbles, jellies
and meringues
Low-fat fruit yoghurt
Biscuits and
cereal bars

CARBOYDRATE FOR FUEL

To get the most out of exercise you need all the basic nutrients – carbohydrate, protein, fat and all the vitamins and minerals. Carbohydrate, protein and fat will give you energy and vitamins and minerals help your body to use this energy to maximise performance.

Carbohydrate and fat are the two main fuels used by muscles during exercise. Fat is the fuel the body mostly uses for low-intensity exercise such as swimming. Carbohydrate is mostly used by the body in high-intensity exercise such as sprinting, or the multiple sprinting seen in field sports like rugby and soccer.

Carbohydrate is stored in the body as glycogen. When you exercise, the body starts to break down glycogen into glucose, which your muscles then use as fuel. Even the leanest athletes already carry enough fat for energy and most sports people need to follow a fairly low- fat (but not fat-free) diet. However, carbohydrate stores in the body are small, so most of the focus for energy should be on maximising the amount of carbohydrate you eat.

Carbohydrates are divided into two main groups – starches (sometimes called complex carbohydrates) and sugars. It is important to eat a variety of carbohydrate foods every day and to include carbohydrate foods at every meal and snack. Sugary carbohydrates can be useful if your energy needs are very high, but be careful of the fat content of foods like biscuits and cakes.

How to eat more carbohydrate when you are training
- Your main meals should all be based around carbohydrate foods e.g. cereal at
- Breakfast, bread as a sandwich at lunchtime and potatoes, pasta or rice at dinner.
- Snack on high-carbohydrate foods in between meals – fruit or wholemeal scones,
- Cereal bars, fresh fruit or fruit smoothies, low-fat yoghurt, fruit breads and dried fruit.
- Use thicker slices of bread when making sandwiches or snacks.
- Add slices of baby potatoes to soups and stews.
- Add pasta and tinned pulses such as butter beans or haricot beans to homemade vegetable soups.
- Go for mashed, baked or boiled potatoes instead of chips, oven chips, roast potatoes or wedges.
- Go for plain, boiled or steamed rice instead of fried rice.
- Chop fresh fruit such as bananas and add to breakfast cereal.
- When choosing salads, include rice and pasta salads as well as other vegetables.

EATING FOR EXERCISE

TIP: Avoid high-fat foods and snacks before exercise – they take longer to leave your stomach and you may feel uncomfortable or nauseous during exercise.

FACT OR FICTION?

Eating lots of protein builds and strengthens muscle.

Fiction: Although protein is needed to help build muscle, it is exercise that actually builds muscle, eating protein without exercise won't make any difference. Good sources of protein are meat, chicken, turkey, fish, eggs and pulses such as beans, peas, lentils and nuts.

BEFORE EXERCISE

Having a good, healthy diet all year round is important before you exercise. You need to make sure you are getting all the nutrients your body needs for good health. When you are exercising you need to focus on your carbohydrate intake to ensure you have enough energy for all the extra activity.

JUST BEFORE EXERCISE

Make sure your glycogen stores are full, by having a high-carbohydrate meal 2-4 hours before exercise. Don't fast before exercise as your glycogen stores will be depleted.

Good pre-exercise meals and snacks include:
- Breakfast cereal with low-fat milk and chopped fruit.
- Fruit smoothie with low-fat yoghurt.
- Toast with jam and low-fat spread.
- Porridge with low-fat milk, sugar or honey and fresh or dried fruit.
- Pasta dishes such as spaghetti bolognaise or pasta salads – avoid cream-based sauces.
- Baked potato with low-fat fillings (baked beans, tuna with low-fat mayonnaise or chilli).
- Sandwich with low-fat spread or low-fat mayonnaise, small amount of meat, chicken or fish.
- Fresh fruit and low-fat yoghurt.
- Cereal bars and yoghurt drink.

Before-exercise meals and snacks should:
- Include a drink to help maintain good hydration.
- Be eaten long enough before exercise to ensure you don't have undigested food in your stomach - but not so far in advance that you start to feel hungry.
- Be low in fat and moderate to low in fibre so that your stomach empties quickly.
- Be high in carbohydrate to maximise glycogen stores.
- Be foods that you are familiar with – don't try anything new just before exercise and especially not before a competition.

AFTER EXERCISE

What you eat after exercise is just as important as what you eat before. During exercise you will use up the glycogen that is stored in your muscles. This glycogen needs to be replaced after exercise so that your muscles are refuelled and ready for your next exercise session. As it takes the body up to 20 hours to rebuild your glycogen stores, it is essential that you start to replace your glycogen immediately after exercise. As you know, glycogen comes from the carbohydrate foods you eat, so you need to make sure you have a high carbohydrate meal or snack immediately after exercise. Studies show that eating within 30 minutes of exercise gives the best results and helps to maximise performance at the next exercise session. You should eat a snack which is high in carbohydrate immediately after exercise – this can be a drink or solid food. This snack should be followed by a high-carbohydrate meal within two hours of finishing exercise. Remember to eat carbohydrate foods at your other meals and snacks throughout the day.

- Use boiled, baked or mashed potatoes instead of chips, roast potatoes or wedges.
- Go for boiled or steamed rice instead of fried.
- Use low-fat mayonnaise or dressings in sandwiches and salads.
- Grill, boil, bake or microwave foods – avoid using the frying pan or deep-fat fryer.
- Go for low-fat milk – preferably low-fat milks that are fortified with vitamins and minerals.
- Use low-fat cheeses such as Camembert, Edam, Feta and Brie, or low-fat cheddar.
- Check the labels of foods for fat – choose foods with a lower fat content.

INDICATION OF BEING DEHYDRATED

Your urine is a good indicator of how much fluid you need – dark urine means you need to drink more fluid and light. Almost clear urine means you are probably well-hydrated.

Good snacks and meals to have after exercise:
- Cereal bar and a glass of milk.
- Pasta dishes made with tomato-based sauces such as spaghetti bolognaise.
- Pasta salads with low-fat mayonnaise – include a small amount of chicken or tuna.
- Sandwich made with lean ham or turkey.
- Low-fat yoghurt and banana or other fresh fruit.
- Fruit smoothie made with low-fat yoghurt.
- Chicken dish with steamed or boiled rice.
- Chilli con carne and rice.
- Baked potato with baked beans.
- Fruit loaf and a yoghurt drink.
- Cheese or baked beans on toast.

Find an Accredited Sports Dietitian

Need some extra help? If you are seriously competing in your chosen sport or want some individual advice on nutrition and athletic performance, an Accredited Sports Dietitian is the best option. An Accredited Sports Dietitian has a special qualification in Sports Nutrition and can evaluate your diet, advise you on your individual nutritional needs and advise on foods for optimizing your sporting performance. A list of Sports Accredited Dietitians is available from the National Coaching and Training Centre website (www.nctc.ul.ie) and the website of the Irish Nutrition and Dietetic Institute (www.indi.ie).

FLUID FOR SPORT

It is well-known that a good intake of fluid before, during and after exercise will help to maximise your performance and help to reduce fatigue. Yet, in spite of its importance, fluid is regularly overlooked or forgotten when people exercise. You need to be well-hydrated before and after exercise for the best performance and this is true for anyone involved in sport – not just the professionals.

Everybody loses water during the day through the skin, kidneys and lungs, and this needs to be replaced by drinking fluids regularly throughout the day. People doing very little exercise need between 2 and 3 litres of fluid every day. When you exercise your need for water is higher because your body sweats to help keep you cool. People who are exercising regularly need between 4 and 8 litres of fluid every day.

It is essential to drink plenty of fluids before, during and after exercise to prevent dehydration. Thirst is not a good indicator of the need for fluid – by the time you feel thirsty you are already slightly dehydrated. Mild dehydration (about 2%) leads to a poorer performance and early fatigue, and more severe dehydration (3-4%) can lead to nausea, vomiting and diarrhoea. Severe dehydration (8% or more) will cause dizziness, weakness and confusion.

Getting your fluid:

- Always bring a drink with you so that you can sip fluid throughout the day.
- Be aware of where you can get fluid – water fountains and coolers, and where you can buy fluid – make sure you always have money to buy drinks and change for vending machines.
- Don't wait until you feel thirsty – drink regularly and frequently during the day.
- Drink enough during the day to have light-coloured urine – dark urine is a sign that you need to drink more.
  Limit the amount of alcohol and caffeine you drink – both will dehydrate you.
- Plan your fluid intake during competitions, matches or events and practice this during your training sessions to find what works best for you.
- Put more water in your stomach than on your head – pouring water over your head does nothing to cool you!

FLUID AND EXERCISE - BEFORE, DURING AND AFTER

Fluid before exercise:
Drink plenty of fluids throughout the day – even on days that you are not training.
Always arrive for training well-hydrated.
Drink 250-500mls of an isotonic drink 30 minutes before training or competition.

Fluid during exercise:
Fluid should be taken for all training or sporting events that last longer than 30 minutes.
Drink 150-200mls of water or isotonic sports drink every 15 minutes while exercising.
If this is not possible drink 300-500mls at half-time.
Avoid fizzy drinks as they may cause stomach upsets.
An isotonic sports drink is recommended if you're training/exercise session lasts longer than 1 hour.

Fluid after exercise:
Start drinking fluid immediately after exercise – don't wait until later.
Good drinks to go for after exercise are water isotonic sports drinks, fruit-drinks (not sugar-free) and soft drinks (not diet). If you don't choose an isotonic sports drink it is useful to eat something salty after exercise as the sodium will speed up rehydration.

WHAT ARE ISOTONIC SPORTS DRINKS

Isotonic drinks are a source of fluid and carbohydrate, can help decrease the risk of dehydration and maximise performance in sports and exercise. The carbohydrate helps to provide energy to exercising muscles. Isotonic sports drinks are available in most supermarkets and local shops, or you can make your own:

200mls squash/cordial (not sugar-free), 800mls water and 1g (pinch) of salt
or 250mls fruit juice, 750mls water and 1g (pinch) of salt.

IRON AND CALCIUM

Some people who are exercising regularly will need more iron or calcium – especially women and teenagers. Make sure you eat some of the following foods regularly:

Good sources of Iron:
Lean red meat
Chicken & turkey
Eggs
Dark green leafy vegetables such as spinach, broccoli and cabbage
Breakfast cereals fortified with iron
Pulses such as beans and lentils
Dried fruit and nuts

Good sources of calcium:
Dairy products – milk, cheese and yoghurt – choose low-fat varieties
Custards and milk puddings (e.g. rice pudding)
Smoothies made with low-fat yoghurt
Soya milk fortified with calcium
Fruit juice fortified with calcium
Green leafy vegetables such as spinach and cabbage
Nuts

TIP: If you are getting your iron from vegetables such as spinach or cabbage, always eat some foods with vitamin C at the same time as it boosts the amount of iron your body absorbs from these foods. Good sources of vitamin C are fresh fruit and vegetables, especially oranges, kiwis and orange juice.

VITAMINS & MINERALS

Everybody needs to get the right amount of vitamins and minerals every day. When it comes to exercise, vitamins and minerals help your body to release energy from the foods you eat, carry oxygen around the body and help with tissue repair. It is important that you have a balanced diet when you exercise – and even if you don't – to ensure you are getting everything you need.

If you eat a balanced diet with foods from all the food groups you will be getting all the vitamins and minerals you need to get the most out of exercise. Choose foods from all five food groups every day.

THE FIVE FOOD GROUPS

Bread cereals and potatoes - this group is the group that provides carbohydrate for energy and fibre. You need 6 or more portions from this group every day. I portion is I slice of bread, I medium potato, I tablespoon of cooked pasta or rice or I bowl of cereal.

Fruit and vegetables - this group provides vitamins, minerals and fibre. You need 5 portions from this group every day. I portion is 3 dessertspoons of cooked vegetables or salad, $^1/_2$ bowl of homemade vegetable soup, I piece of fresh fruit or $^1/_2$ glass of pure fruit juice.

Milk, cheese & yoghurt - this group provides calcium. You need 3 dairy portions of dairy every day, and 5 a day during your teens. I portion is I glass of milk, I yoghurt or Ioz of hard cheese. Choose low-fat varieties.

Meat, fish and alternatives - this group gives you protein. You need 2 portions from this group every day. I portion is 2oz/50g meat, chicken or turkey (this is about the size of half a large chicken breast), 3oz/75g fish, 2 eggs and 6 tablespoons of beans, peas or lentils.

Fats, sugars and oils - this group includes spreads and butters, oils and confectionery, sweets, biscuits and cakes. Although we need some fat every day, we just need a small amount. This food group should only be eaten occasionally.

DO I NEED A SUPPLEMENT?
If you are following a balanced diet you don't need to take vitamin or mineral supplements. Some people take supplements if they are not following a balanced diet, but it is better to get your nutrients from your diet. It is best not to take large doses of any one vitamin or mineral as these can cause problems. If you are unsure about whether or not you need a supplement for exercise, contact a Sports Accredited Dietitian.

READING LABELS

The nutrition labels on foods will give you good information about the amount of carbohydrate, protein and fat the food contains. Learning how to read a food label can help you make better food choices when you are exercising.

There are usually two columns of figures on a nutrition label. One column will tell you how much of each nutrient is found in a normal portion of the food, eg. the amount of fat found in one biscuit in a packet.

The second column will tell you how much of each nutrient is found in 100g of the product. The 100g column is very useful as you can use it to compare different foods with different portion sizes.

WHAT TO LOOK FOR ON A FOOD LABEL:
How much energy? On a food label, energy is given as kcal (calories) or kJ (kilojoules which is just another way of measuring energy). This section is useful if you want to watch the amount of calories you're eating.

Is it high or low in fat? To be low in fat a food must have less than 3g of fat per 100g or 100ml of the food. It is best to choose low-fat foods regularly. A food with more than 20g of fat per 100g or 100ml of the product is a high-fat food. These should only be eaten occasionally.

Is it high or low in sugar? To be low in sugar there must be less than 5g of sugar per 100g or 100ml of the product. A food with 10g or more is a high-sugar food. High-sugar foods can be useful as a quick source of carbohydrate for exercise, but it is better to choose more complex carbohydrates like pasta and bread.

Is it high or low in salt? A food with more than 1.5g of sodium is high in salt. A food with less than 0.1g of sodium is a low-salt food.

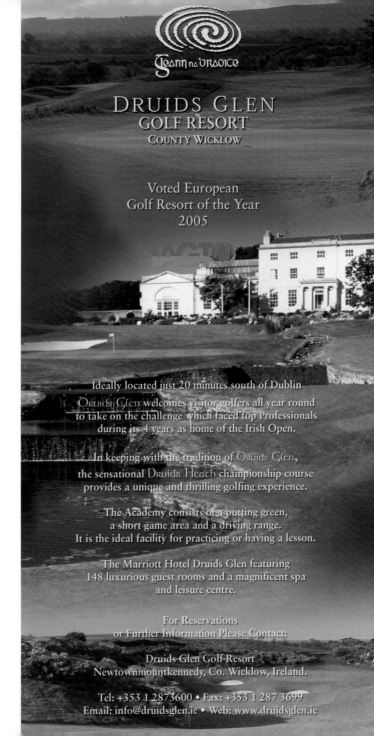

Q&A

Favourite restaurant:
Café Bar Deli

Favourite sporting hero:
DJ Carey

3 things I always have in my fridge:
Milk, Actimel, water

Favourite place in the world to visit:
Brazil

People would be surprised to know:
I have a bad temper

Brian was born in Dublin and educated at Blackrock College and University College Dublin. He played for Ireland Schools and Ireland Under-21's. He won his first cap on the tour to Australia in June 1999 and has been ever-present since then. In the summer of 2001 he played in all three tests for the Lions and scored a brilliant hat-trick of tries in the 2002 Six Nations game against Scotland. He captained Ireland for the first time when winning his 31st cap in 2002 and took over as captain of the squad for the 2004 Six Nations. He was named as Ireland's first British & Irish Lions skipper since Ciaran Fitzgerald. He played in the first test, but had his shoulder dislocated and took no further part in the remaining games. Brian is currently recovering from that injury and hopes to be back playing in December 2005.

SPAGHETTI BOLOGNESE

BRIAN O'DRISCOL

SERVES 2

200g lean mince beef
1 tin chopped tomatoes
1 small onion, finely chopped
1tsp dried basil
1tsp dried oregano
Salt and pepper
150g spaghetti

1. Dry-fry the meat and onion until the meat is cooked.
2. Add the tinned tomatoes and the seasoning.
3. Cook the spaghetti in plenty of salted boiling water until al dente. Drain.
4. Serve the spaghetti with the bolognese sauce.

NUTRIENT ANALYSIS FOR ONE SERVING

Fat	11.2g	**Energy**	444kcal	**Sodium**	.1g
Carbs	57.9g	**Protein**	31.6g	**Fibre**	4.5g

POST-MATCH
FAVOURITE
POST-MATCH

STEAK WITH BAKED POTATO & SOUR CREAM

SERVES 1

1 6-8oz striploin steak
2 baking potatoes, washed and scrubbed
A little olive oil
Salt
Sour cream
$1/4$ cup chives, finely chopped

To serve
Green salad with balsamic dressing

1. Preheat the oven to 190ºC/gas mark 5.
2. Prick the potatoes all over with a fork. Cover the potatoes with a little oil and salt. Place on a baking sheet and bake for 45 minutes until cooked.
3. Grill the steak until it is medium rare.
4. Mix the sour cream with the chives.
5. Make a slit in the baked potatoes and top with the sour cream mixture. Serve the steak with the baked potatoes and salad.

NUTRIENT ANALYSIS FOR ONE SERVING

Fat	27g	**Energy**	638kcal	**Sodium**	.1g
Carbs	46g	**Protein**	57g	**Fibre**	4g

Q&A

Favourite restaurant:
Conor, Stranmills, Belfast

Favourite sporting hero:
Roger Federer

3 things I always have in my fridge:
Mayo, cheese, full-fat milk

Ever tried the Atkins diet?
No, I'm trying to put on weight!

Party piece:
Playing Pink Panther on the saxophone

Tommy was educated at Royal School Armagh. A talented Gaelic Footballer who played Minor Football for Monaghan, he first played for Ireland at Under-21 level and was a regular for them for the last couple of years. However, after playing in just two games in the Under-21 World Cup in Scotland in 2004, he sustained a shoulder injury which forced him to miss the rest of the tournament as Ireland progressed to the final. Fit again, he became a regular in the Ulster side last season and his performances for them in the Celtic League and Heineken Cup saw him brought into the Ireland side. He won his first full cap last November against the United States and he marked the occasion by scoring his first international try. He scored his second try for Ireland in the first test against Japan during the summer, where he played in both tests.

CREAMY CHICKEN TAGLIATELLE

SERVES 4

450g boneless, skinless chicken breasts, cut into strips
Dash of olive oil
1 x 500g jar Country French Chicken Tonight
400g tagliatelle pasta

To serve
Salad
Crusty bread

1. Pan-fry the chicken in a little olive oil until golden.
2. Stir in the sauce, cover and simmer for 20 minutes or until the chicken is fully cooked.
3. Cook tagliatelle in plenty of salted, boiling water until just tender. Drain well and divide among pasta bowls.
4. Top with chicken sauce and serve immediately with salad and crusty bread.

NUTRIENT ANALYSIS FOR ONE SERVING

Fat	8g	Energy	517kcal	Sodium	.5g
Carbs	66g	Protein	49g	Fibre	0g

POST-MATCH **FAVOURITE** POST-MATCH

PEKING DUCK

SERVES 6

1 duck (4 to 5 lbs), cleaned and giblets
removed
14 cups water
4tbsp honey
4 slices ginger, 1/8 inch thick
1/2 cup white vinegar
1/2 cup pale dry sherry
1 packet lumpia wrappers
(Chinese pancakes)
24 pieces green onion stems
2 oz. Chinese parsley or coriander
Chinese Hoisin sauce

To serve:
Fried rice

1. Rinse duck and pat dry.
2. Put water, honey, ginger, vinegar and sherry into a large pot or wok and bring
to a boil.
3. Place duck into the pot and ladle boiling liquid over it for 2 minutes.
4. Remove duck and pat dry with absorbent paper. Hang or leave to air-dry in a
cool, breezy place for 5-8 hours.
5. Remove scum and fat from liquid and freeze for future use.
6. Heat oven to 350° degrees. Put duck directly on oven rack, breast side up. On
a lower oven rack, place a foil-lined roasting pan filled with an inch of water to
catch the drippings.
7. Roast for 30 minutes or until duck looks crispy. For crispier duck, fry the
whole duck for 15 minutes.
8. Remove the skin and debone the duck. Cut the skin into 1 x 2 inch pieces and
shred the meat with scissors. Arrange on a heated platter being careful not to let
the juices wet the crispy skin.
9. Heat the lumpia wrappers and place in a napkin-lined basket to keep warm.
Put hoisin sauce, green onions and coriander in separate serving bowls.
10. To eat, spread pancakes with hoisin, top with shredded meat and skin, a few
green onion slivers and some coriander. Fold and eat with your hands with a side
serving of fried rice.

NUTRIENT ANALYSIS FOR ONE SERVING

Fat	32g	**Energy**	647kcal	**Sodium**	.4g
Carbs	13g	**Protein**	79g	**Fibre**	1g

"Remember that rugby is a team game; all 14 of you make sure you pass the ball to Jonah!"

(fax to the All Blacks before the 1995 World Cup semi-final)

HRM
building relationships

recruiting teams since 1992.

Q&A

Favourite restaurant:
Elephant & Castle

Favourite sporting hero:
Daly Thompson

3 things I always have in my fridge:
Milk, sliced meat, butter

Party piece:
Don't normally have one, but can be coaxed (easily) into singing

Worse date:
Can't remember, married too long!

SHANE BYRNE

Shane was born in Dublin, brought up in Aughrim, County Wicklow and educated at Blackrock College and Dundalk RTC. The Saracens hooker had to wait until June 2001 to win his first cap after many years of being involved with the Irish squad. Over the next couple of seasons, Shane, nicknamed "Munch", won several caps mainly as a replacement. He came into the front row when prolonged injury kept Keith Wood sidelined in 2003. He stepped centre stage when Wood retired and scored two tries in Ireland's Six Nations win over Wales in February 2004. Apart from the 55-6 autumn test win over the US Eagles in which he was an unused replacement, Shane has started the majority of Ireland's recent tests, playing a large part in making Ireland's lineout arguably the best in the world. The 34-year-old was deservedly included in Sir Clive Woodward's British & Irish Lions squad for the summer tour to New Zealand, where he played in all three test matches.

PRE-MATCH
FAVOURITE
PRE-MATCH

CHICKEN & NOODLE STIR-FRY

SERVES 4

2tbsp olive oil
2 cloves garlic, crushed
1.5cm piece ginger, grated
1 carrot, thinly sliced
100g broccoli florets
100g mushrooms, sliced
2 onions, chopped
1/4 cup oyster sauce
1tsp brown sugar
few drops
sesame oil
600g egg noodles, soaked in hot water and drained
500g cooked chicken breast fillets, shredded

1. Heat the oil in a wok or large frying pan. Stir-fry the garlic, onion and ginger until aromatic.
2. Add the shredded chicken and stir-fry for 3 minutes.
3. Add the carrot, broccoli and mushrooms and cook for 2 minutes.
4. Blend in the oyster sauce, sugar and oil. Stir-fry for 1 minute. Toss through the noodles and stir-fry until heated through. Divide between bowls and serve immediately.

NUTRIENT ANALYSIS FOR ONE SERVING

| **Fat** | 23g | **Energy** | 858kcal | **Sodium** | .5g |
| **Carbs** | 117g | **Protein** | 53g | **Fibre** | 9g |

POST-MATCH **FAVOURITE** POST-MATCH

BEEF STROGANOFF

SERVES 4

500g blade, round or fillet steak, sliced with all visible fat trimmed off
2 onions, sliced
1 clove garlic, crushed
250g mushrooms, sliced
1 x 425g can chopped tomatoes
1/2 cup red wine
1tbsp tomato paste
2 tomatoes, diced
1tbsp chopped parsley
Freshly ground pepper to taste
1/2 cup light sour cream or low-fat natural yogurt

To serve
Boiled brown rice
Crusty bread

1. Lightly brush a non-stick frying pan with olive oil. Add half of the beef and brown well over medium heat, stirring frequently. Remove to a plate.
2. Brown remaining meat with onions and garlic. Return first batch of meat to pan with mushrooms. Cook, stirring for 3 minutes.
3. Blend in tomatoes, wine and tomato paste. Bring to the boil. Reduce heat. Simmer, uncovered for 10 to 15 minutes, adding a little water as required.
4. Stir through tomatoes, parsley, mushrooms and black pepper. Simmer mixture for a further 5 minutes and blend in the sour cream. Bring back to the boil.
5. Serve with boiled brown rice and crusty bread.

NUTRIENT ANALYSIS FOR ONE SERVING

Fat	15g	**Energy**	299kcal	**Sodium**	.2g
Carbs	7g	**Protein**	30g	**Fibre**	3g

Q&A

Favourite restaurant:
Hungry Monk, Greystones

Ever played with fear of injury?
Yes

Party piece:
Singing Louis Armstrong songs

Bill McLaren or Jim Sherwin?
Bill McLaren

Worst date?
I've been lucky—no bad ones!

Reggie was educated at Presentation College, Bray. In November '97 he won his first cap as a replacement against Canada. The following month, Reggie started his first international against Italy, and went on to win another five caps by the end of 1998. However he had to wait until the 1999 tour to Australia to add to his tally — coming on as a replacement in both tests. The following season he played in the '99 World Cup game against Argentina, but did not win another cap until playing in both tests in the summer of '02 against New Zealand. Since then he has been virtually ever-present playing in 32 of the last 39 tests. He has been a stalwart for his province Leinster over the last decade and has over 100 caps to his name. He toured Japan with Ireland in the summer and made appearances as a replacement in both test matches.

PRE-MATCH
FAVOURITE
PRE-MATCH

PENNE WITH CREAMY CHICKEN & SUNDRIED TOMATO SAUCE

SERVES 4

500g penne pasta
250g chicken breast fillet, chopped
1 onion, sliced
2tbsp olive oil
200g (1 cup) sun-dried tomatoes, chopped
$1/2$ cup cream
2tbsp shredded basil
Salt and pepper to taste

To serve
Salad
Crusty bread

1. Cook penne in plenty of boiling, salted water until tender. Drain well.
2. Melt the butter in a large frying pan and sauté the onion over medium heat until soft and translucent.
3. Add the chopped chicken and cook over high heat until browned and cooked through.
4. Add the sundried tomatoes, cream and seasonings. Reduce heat. Simmer gently for 3–5 minutes or until the cream has reduced slightly.
5. Add the penne to the pan and stir gently to coat well. Divide into bowls and garnish with the shredded basil. Serve immediately with salad and crusty bread.

NUTRIENT ANALYSIS FOR ONE SERVING

Fat	42g	Energy	804kcal	Sodium	.5g
Carbs	74g	Protein	37g	Fibre	0.7g

POST-MATCH
FAVOURITE
POST-MATCH

MONKFISH WITH KING PRAWNS & ROASTED VEGETABLES

SERVES 4

4 monkfish fillets
16 king prawns, cleaned
2 red peppers, deseeded and sliced
2 red onions, peeled and quartered
200g mushrooms, wiped and halved
1 large aubergine, sliced into rounds and halved
2 cloves of garlic, crushed
Olive oil
Juice of $^1/_2$ lemon
Balsamic vinegar

1. Preheat the oven to 180°C/ gas mark 4.
2. Spread the red peppers, onions, aubergine and mushrooms out onto a baking sheet and drizzle with olive oil. Bake for about 20 minutes and then drizzle with balsamic vinegar.
3. In the meantime heat a little olive oil in a heavy-based frying pan. Add the garlic and lemon juice, bring to boil and then add the monkfish. Fry for about 4 minutes on each side or until cooked through, adding the king prawns for the last 3 minutes and cooking until opaque.
4. Arrange the roasted vegetables on a plate and top with the monkfish and prawns.

NUTRIENT ANALYSIS FOR ONE SERVING

Fat	6g	Energy	302kcal	Sodium	.4g
Carbs	3g	Protein	60g	Fibre	2g

WORKING TOGETHER WE WORK OUR BEST.

As any sportsman or woman will tell you, a well-run team can achieve a great deal more than the individuals who form it. You'll see the same principle at work in Hibernian: all of our staff rely on each other for strong support and honest feedback - so that our customers can rely on us for service that meets their expectations, and products that meet their needs.

HIBERNIAN
an **AVIVA** company

Hibernian Life & Pensions, 60/63 Dawson Street, Dublin 2. Tel: (01) 617 8000 www.hibernian.ie
Hibernian Life & Pensions Limited is regulated by the Financial Regulator.

Q&A

Favourite sporting hero:
Lance Armstrong, an inspiration to any athlete

Party piece:
Marinating my special burgers for annual BBQ

One thing could not live without:
Coffee, my one true vice. I love it!

People would be surprised to know:
I love to surf, am not very good at it but getting better!

If I wasn't a rugby player:
I'd be an architect, my dream job

Gordon was educated at Clongowes Wood College and helped the school win the Leinster Senior Cup in 1998. He made his Ireland 'A' debut in February '99 and then got called into Ireland's RWC Squad as a replacement and won his first cap against Romania. Making up for the disappointment of being left out of Ireland's 2003 RWC squad, D'Arcy turned in some stunning performances in the 2004 Six Nations tournament, most notably in the 19-13 Twickenham defeat of England and his two-try performance in the Triple Crown clinching win against Scotland. He won the RBS Six Nations Player of the Tournament and went on to win the IRUPA Players' Player of the Year 2004 to crown a magnificent season. His 2004/05 season was hampered by injury but he was rewarded in April when he was named alongside five other Leinster team mates in the 2005 British & Irish Lions squad.

CHICKEN WITH ROASTED ROOT VEGETABLES

GORDON D'ARCY

SERVES 4

200g parsnip, cut into chunks
4 carrots, cut into chunks
2 large sweet potatoes, peeled and cubed
2tbsp chilli oil
Salt and pepper
200g broccoli, cut into florets
4 chicken breasts
4 cloves of garlic
Juice of 1 lemon
1tbsp chopped fresh thyme
1tbsp chopped fresh rosemary
2tbsp olive oil

1. Preheat the oven to 220°C/gas mark 8. Lightly oil a large roasting tin.
2. Put the parsnip, carrots and sweet potatoes into a large roasting tin.
Drizzle the vegetables with the chilli oil, add salt and pepper and bake for
30-40 minutes.
3. While the vegetables are roasting, add the lemon juice to the chicken breasts.
Wrap each breast in kitchen foil and season with the fresh herbs. Drizzle over
the olive oil and leave a whole garlic clove in each pouch. Roast the chicken
breasts in the oven for 30 minutes until cooked.
4. Boil the broccoli until just tender.
5. Serve the chicken breasts with the roasted vegetables and broccoli.

NUTRIENT ANALYSIS FOR ONE SERVING

Fat	12g	Energy	385kcal	Sodium	.3g
Carbs	24g	Protein	46g	Fibre	5g

POST-MATCH
FAVOURITE
POST-MATCH

BEEF FILLET WRAPPED IN PARMA HAM WITH ONION & WILD MUSHROOM STUFFING

SERVES 4

4 fillet steaks
4 Parma ham slices

Stuffing
1 large onion, finely chopped
100g wild mushrooms, chopped
Small bunch of parsley, chopped
3 cups breadcrumbs
50g butter, melted
Salt and pepper

Baked red onions
4 whole red onions, peeled
4 rashers of smoked bacon
Large knob of butter
Salt

To serve
Mushroom and black pepper sauce
Baked baby potatoes

1. Preheat the oven to 200ºC/gas mark 6.
2. Make the stuffing first. Combine the chopped onion, wild mushrooms, parsley, breadcrumbs and melted butter in a bowl. Season well.
3. Put the fillet steaks into a roasting tin and layer the stuffing onto each fillet. Wrap each steak with a slice of Parma ham and roast them in the oven for 30 minutes until the steaks are tender and cooked.
4. Rub the butter onto the red onions, wrap in the smoked bacon and season with salt. Cover with foil and cook for 30 minutes.
5. Serve the steak fillets with the roasted onions, baked baby potatoes and mushroom and black pepper sauce.

NUTRIENT ANALYSIS FOR ONE SERVING

Fat	35g	**Energy**	803kcal	**Sodium**	.2g
Carbs	76g	**Protein**	51g	**Fibre**	5g

Q&A

Favourite restaurant:
Drum & Monkey

Favourite sporting hero:
Stuart Pearce

If a streaker tried to tackle me:
I'd go for their tackle!

Charlize Theron or Halle Berry?
Charlize Theron

Party piece:
A disappearing clothes act (same as my brother Guy)

Simon Easterby was educated at Ampleforth College and won his first full cap against Scotland in February 2000 and then became a regular in the side, being ever-present for the remainder of the Six Nations competition. Simon then played in all three of the games during the summer tour but missed all of the following season due to injury. He returned for the game against Scotland in September '01. After Ireland's defeat he won a cap as a replacement against Samoa in November '01. In 2002 he played a part in the first ten of Ireland's games and has been a regular starter ever since in the number 6 jersey. Simon is a vital component of the Llanelli Scarlets team and is currently team captain. He was also called up for the British & Irish Lions tour to New Zealand and went on to play in two of the three tests.

CAPPELLETTI PASTA WITH CHICKEN & VEGETABLES

SIMON EASTERBY

SERVES 4

250g boneless, skinless chicken breast, cooked and diced
500g cappelletti pasta (pasta filled with ham and cheese)
2tbsp olive oil
1 red onion, finely chopped
4 tomatoes, chopped
1/2 cup water
1tbsp tomato paste
1 green pepper, seeded and sliced
100g mange tout
Salt and pepper to taste
1/4 cup shredded basil leaves
Shaved parmesan cheese

1. Cook pasta in plenty of salted, boiling water until tender. Drain well and set aside.
2. Heat oil in a large frying pan and sauté onion and garlic until onion is tender. Add chicken, tomatoes, peppers, water and tomato paste.
3. Bring to the boil. Reduce heat and simmer for 5 minutes. Season to taste.
4. Add pasta to the pan with the basil and mange tout. Toss over medium heat for 2 minutes. Serve immediately sprinkled with parmesan.

Note. If preferred you could use one 425g can of tomatoes instead of fresh tomatoes and omit the water and tomato paste.

NUTRIENT ANALYSIS FOR ONE SERVING

Fat	19g	Energy	363kcal	Sodium	.3g
Carbs	19g	Protein	31g	Fibre	4g

POST-MATCH **FAVOURITE** POST-MATCH

CHINESE HOT & SOUR SOUP

SERVES 4

6 cups chicken stock
125g pork fillets, thinly sliced
60g chicken, finely chopped
8 king prawns, cleaned
$^1/_4$ cup long grain rice
$^1/_2$ cup mushrooms, sliced
$^1/_2$ cup bamboo shoots
$^1/_2$ cup carrots, sliced into thin strips
$^1/_2$ cup peas

$^1/_4$ cup vinegar
2tbsp soy sauce
1 egg, beaten
1tsp sesame oil

To serve
6 shallots, chopped
1 fresh chilli, chopped (optional)

1. Bring stock to the boil in a large saucepan. Add the pork, chicken and rice. Reduce heat and simmer for 5 minutes.
2. Stir in the mushrooms, bamboo shoots, carrots and peas. Simmer for a further 5 minutes.
3. Blend in combined vinegar and soy sauce. Add the prawns and simmer for a further 3 minutes or until rice is tender and the prawns are opaque. Remove from heat.
4. Stir in the beaten egg and sesame oil. Serve sprinkled with chopped shallots and chilli.

NUTRIENT ANALYSIS FOR ONE SERVING

Fat	8g	Energy	323kcal	Sodium	.5g
Carbs	19g	Protein	44g	Fibre	3g

36   EATING TO WIN

For OUR GAME
you need to
PUT IT IN
ISOTONIC sports fuel

club
Energise
SPORT
ISOTONIC SPORTS FUEL

 IRUPA IRISH RUGBY UNION PLAYERS ASSOCIATION **Official Sports Drink of IRUPA**

Q&A

Favourite restaurant:
Lyon's, Mountshannon, Co. Clare

Favourite sporting hero:
Roy Keane

3 things I always have in my fridge:
Milk, apple juice, butter

Party piece:
Sleeping in the corner

Chinese or Italian food?
Italian

Anthony, a son of former International Brendan, was born in Limerick and educated at St. Munchins College and Mid-West Business Institute. In 1995 he won his first cap against England. He went on to play in the three remaining Five-Nations games. In January '97 he played against Italy and won his ninth international cap when coming on as a replacement for Eric Miller against England. During the 1999/00 season he returned to the Irish Senior side and he was ever-present for the 2000 Six Nations. During the summer 2000 Americas tour he played in the tests against Argentina and Canada and has been first choice number 8 since then. He captained the side in the November 2001 test against Samoa at Lansdowne Road and scored a try against France in the 2004 RBS Six Nations opener in Paris. He followed up with another in the game against Wales in Lansdowne Road. He is Munster's most capped player, leading try-scorer and also holds the record for most Heineken Cup matches in the history of the tournament.

ANTHONY FOLEY

PRE-MATCH **FAVOURITE** PRE-MATCH

POACHED EGGS, BAKED BEANS & TOAST

PER PERSON

2 eggs
2 thick slices of toast
Butter
100g baked beans
Salt and freshly cracked black pepper

Serve with:
Pancakes & maple syrup
Apple juice
Fresh coffee

1. In a shallow frying pan, bring 5cm of water to the boil. Turn off the heat and add the eggs at once. To minimise the spreading of the whites, break the eggs directly into the water, carefully opening the two halves of the shells at the water surface so that the eggs slide into the water. Cover the pan with a tight-fitting lid. Leave the eggs to cook undisturbed in the water for about 3 minutes. The eggs are cooked when the whites are opaque.
2. Remove the eggs from the pan with a slotted spoon and drain on a clean tea towel.
3. Butter the toast and top with baked beans and poached eggs. Season to taste.
4. Serve along with hot pancakes and maple syrup, pure apple juice and fresh coffee.

NUTRIENT ANALYSIS FOR ONE SERVING

Fat	18g	Energy	358kcal	Sodium	.6g
Carbs	30g	Protein	21g	Fibre	8.4g

POST-MATCH **FAVOURITE** POST-MATCH

ANTHONY FOLEY

PASTA SHELLS WITH FRESH TUNA & TOMATO SAUCE

SERVES 4

500g pasta shells
250g fresh tuna
2tbsp olive oil
2 tins chopped tomatoes
2 cloves garlic, crushed
2tbsp pitted
black olives
2tbsp fresh herbs, chopped

Salt and freshly ground pepper
to taste

To serve
Shaved parmesan cheese
Salad
Crusty bread

1. Cook pasta shells in plenty of salted, boiling water until tender. Drain well and set aside.
2. Heat olive oil in a frying pan and cook tuna over medium heat for 5-7 minutes or until cooked. Remove from pan and set aside.
3. Heat the remaining tablespoon of olive oil in the frying pan and add the tomatoes and garlic. Bring to the boil. Reduce heat and simmer for 2-3 minutes until slightly reduced.
4. Flake tuna with a fork. Add to the tomato mixture. Stir through the olives, herbs and seasonings. Gently toss through hot pasta to coat.
5. Serve immediately topped with parmesan cheese if desired, accompanied by a salad and crusty bread.

Note. Substitute fresh tuna with one 425g can of tuna in brine, drained, if fresh fish isn't available.

NUTRIENT ANALYSIS FOR ONE SERVING

Fat	15g	Energy	527kcal	Sodium	.2g
Carbs	73g	Protein	30g	Fibre	.4g

Q&A

Favourite restaurant:
Larkins, Garrykennedy, Co. Tipperary

Favourite sporting hero:
Michael Schumacher

3 things I always have in my fridge:
Cheese, milk, ham

People would be surprised to know:
How nice I am

**If I wasn't a professional
rugby player:**
I'd be a farmer

John was born in Limerick and was educated at Doon CBS. He did not begin his rugby career until the age of 18 when he joined Limerick club side Bruff. He moved from there to Shannon and after playing two seasons with the Under-20s he helped the club win the All-Ireland League in 1995. He then moved to New Zealand for two years. After his return he was called into the Ireland Senior squad for the first time for the summer tour to South Africa in 1998. He didn't win his first cap until 2000 against Scotland but has been first choice ever since. He has over 100 appearances for Munster and toured New Zealand with the British & Irish Lions in the summer.

PRE-MATCH **FAVOURITE** PRE-MATCH

CHICKEN WITH POTATO CAKES

SERVES 4

1tbsp olive oil
2tbsp lemon juice
1tbsp flour
1/2 tsp salt
1/2 tsp paprika
4 skinless chicken breasts

Potato cakes
700g ready-made mash
8oz plain flour
4 eggs
1tbsp olive oil

To serve
Selection of steamed green vegetables

1. Preheat the oven to 180ºC/gas mark 4.
2. Combine the olive oil, lemon juice, flour, salt and paprika. Coat the chicken breasts with the mixture and grill on both sides until cooked.
3. For the potato cakes, place the mash, egg and flour into a large bowl and beat together until combined. Add more flour if required to form a stiff dough.
4. Fry the potato cakes on a heated frying pan for 1 minute on either side.
5. Serve the chicken breasts with the potato cakes and green vegetables.

NUTRIENT ANALYSIS FOR ONE SERVING

Fat	25g	**Energy**	733kcal	**Sodium**	.5g
Carbs	76g	**Protein**	57g	**Fibre**	4g

JOHN HAYES

POST-MATCH
FAVOURITE
POST-MATCH

BAKED HAM, CABBAGE & CHAMP

SERVES 4

Baked ham
2 1/2 kg ham, soaked in cold water for
24 hours
2 onions, quartered
A few cloves
A few black peppercorns
1 bay leaf
2tbsp English mustard
110g dark brown sugar

Champ
125g spring onions, chopped
300ml milk
6 potatoes
Salt and pepper
75g butter

To serve
Cabbage

1. Preheat the oven to 190ºC/gas mark 5. Place the soaked ham in a large pan, with the onions, cloves, peppercorns and bay leaf.
2. Cover with water, bring to the boil and skim away any impurities.
3. Leave the ham to simmer, allowing 20 minutes per 450g.
4. Once cooked, remove the ham from the pan and stand for 10-15 minutes before peeling away the skin.
5. Brush the ham with mustard and sprinkle well with the brown sugar.
6. Bake the ham for 30-40 minutes taking care to baste the ham with pan juices.
7. Once the ham is golden, remove from the oven and rest for 15-30 minutes before carving.
8. Then prepare the champ. Simmer the chopped spring onions in the milk until soft. Boil the potatoes in salted water until just cooked, then mash.
9. Add the onions and their milk to the mash and season with salt and pepper.
10. Serve the ham sliced with the champ and cabbage.

NUTRIENT ANALYSIS FOR ONE SERVING

Fat	35g	**Energy**	931kcal	**Sodium**	.6g
Carbs	62g	**Protein**	99g	**Fibre**	2g

When it comes to sport we've got the recipe

ake a mix of

GAA, Soccer & Rugby,

dd it to Ireland's

rightest news coverage

njoyed by over

26,000 people

etween Breakfast

Tea every day

catering for 426,000 readers every day!

Q&A

Favourite restaurant:
Locks, Portobello, Dublin

Favourite sporting hero:
Bobby "Dazzler" George—what an entertainer!

If a streaker tried to tackle me:
In NZ a streaker ran up behind me and tapped me on the shoulder. I looked at him. He said "Hello Denis" and ran off

3 things I always have in my fridge:
Strawberries, Red Stripe beer, orange juice

People would be surprised to know:
I watch no sport on TV at all

Denis was born in Dublin and whilst at St. Mary's College played on the Ireland Schools Triple Crown winning side in 1993. He made his Ireland Under-21 debut against Wales in February 1995 and the following season was on the Under-21 Triple Crown side. In February '97 he was promoted from the 'A' side to the Senior squad as a replacement for James Topping. He celebrated his debut with a try against Wales and held his place for the games against England and Scotland. During the 1997/98 season he won nine caps. He missed a couple of seasons through injury, which affected his form and returned in February 2000. He remained in the side until injuring his Achilles against Australia during the World Cup in November 2003 and did not return to the Ireland side until the game against South Africa in November 2004. He remained as first choice throughout the 2005 RBS Six Nations Championship and was selected to tour New Zealand with the British & Irish Lions.

BAKED SWEET POTATOES WITH FRESH TUNA STEAKS

DENIS HICKIE

PRE-MATCH FAVOURITE PRE-MATCH

SERVES 4

4 sweet potatoes
3 cups green beans
Juice of 1 lemon
4 tuna steaks
Salt and pepper

1. Preheat the oven to 200ºC/gas mark 6.
2. Wash and scrub the sweet potatoes.
3. Place them in the preheated oven and bake for 40 minutes.
4. Pour the lemon juice over the tuna steaks and season well.
5. Grill or fry the tuna steaks for 20 minutes until cooked.
6. Boil or steam the green beans for 10 minutes until just tender.
7. Serve the tuna with the baked sweet potatoes and green beans.

NUTRIENT ANALYSIS FOR ONE SERVING

Fat	13g	Energy	312kcal	Sodium	.1g
Carbs	26g	Protein	23g	Fibre	.7g

POST-MATCH
FAVOURITE
POST-MATCH

PEPPERONI & HAM PIZZA

SERVES 2

2 ready-made pizza bases

Tomato sauce
2tbsp olive oil
1 medium onion, finely chopped
2 cloves of garlic, crushed
1tsp dried oregano
1 tin chopped tomatoes
1tbsp tomato paste
1tbsp sugar
Salt and pepper

Topping
120g mozzarella
50g parmesan cheese
10 slices of pepperoni
10 slices of ham

To serve
Green salad

1. *Make the tomato sauce by frying the onion and garlic in olive oil until pale and translucent.*
2. *Add the chopped tomatoes, tomato paste, dried oregano and sugar.*
3. *Season to taste.*
4. *Bring to the boil, then reduce heat and simmer until sauce is reduced by half.*
5. *Layer the tomato sauce onto the 2 pizza bases.*
6. *Sprinkle the cheese on top of the pizzas and divide the pepperoni and ham slices on top.*
7. *Bake in the oven for 10-12 minutes until crisp and the cheese has melted.*

NUTRIENT ANALYSIS FOR ONE SERVING

Fat	51g	**Energy**	799kcal	**Sodium**	.5g
Carbs	46g	**Protein**	41g	**Fibre**	.4g

BDO Simpson Xavier
Sports Unit

Give Your
Finances a
Sporting
Chance

If you are engaged in the world of sport you will regularly be faced with challenges and opportunitie

In the constantly evolving sports business environment there will be many similar financial challenges and opportunities.

BDO Simpson Xavier is the first Irish tax and financial consultancy firm to have a dedicated sports unit to advise sports professionals, associations and enterprises.

We understand, better than most, the financial issues our sporting clients face having worked with a myriad of sports professionals and associations over the years.

The services we provide and the areas we cover include:

- Tax Structuring
- Tax Efficient Exploitation of Image Rights
- Retirement Planning
- Investment Advice
- Tax Exemptions for Sporting Bodies
- Financial Reporting and Compliance

- Sportspersons Tax Reli
- International Tax Advic
- Personal Wealth Mana
- Inheritance Tax Plannin
- VAT Advice
- Tax Efficient Funding fo Sports Organisation

So if you are looking for professionals with a proven track record give us a call.

For further information about how we can help you please contact:
Ciarán Medlar
Head of BDO Simpson Xavier Sports Unit
Tel: 0 470 0271
Email: cmedlar@bdosx.ie
Web: www.bdosx.ie

BDO Simpson Xavier
Tax Advisers

Q&A

Favourite restaurant:
Gallagher's Seafood Restaurant,
Bunratty, Co. Clare

Favourite sporting hero:
Michael Jordan

If a streaker tried to tackle me:
I'd leg it!

Party piece:
A poor effort at a song!

Worse date:
None, they've all been great!

Marcus was educated at St. Munchin's College and Limerick Institute of Technology. He won his first cap on the summer tour of 2000 when coming on against the United States. Marcus then had to wait over two years for his second which came in November '02 against Fiji.
He then won three caps as a replacement before returning to the starting line-up against France in March '03. He became a regular in the side playing in eight of the next ten internationals. He did win caps as a replacement in the final three games of that tournament, but due to injury he missed the opening three games of the 2004 Six-Nations. Marcus has since won another 10 caps as a replacement and he started last November against the United States and twice against Japan during the summer. He is a regular in the Munster team and has been part of some outstanding victories and scored an out standing individual try against Stade Francais in the Heineken Cup quarter final in 2004.

PRE-MATCH
FAVOURITE
PRE-MATCH

WHOLEMEAL PANCAKES WITH CHOCOLATE SPREAD

SERVES 6

350g wholemeal flour
Pinch of salt
2 extra large eggs
500ml milk
Oil for frying

To serve
Chocolate spread

1. *Place the flour and salt in a large mixing bowl. Mix.*
2. *Make a hollow in the centre and break in the eggs. Stir to combine.*
3. *Gradually add the milk, beating until the batter is smooth.*
4. *Leave to stand for 30 minutes.*
5. *Heat a little oil in a heavy-based frying pan and add a soup ladle full of pancake batter. Cook until bubbles start to form on the top, then turn over and cook the side. Repeat until all the batter is used up.*
6. *Serve spread with a light smear of chocolate spread.*

NUTRIENT ANALYSIS FOR ONE SERVING

Fat	9g	Energy	283kcal	Sodium	.4g
Carbs	41g	Protein	12g	Fibre	5g

MARCUS HORAN

POST-MATCH **FAVOURITE** POST-MATCH

TRADITIONAL ROAST CHICKEN

SERVES 4 - 6

6 potatoes, cut into wedges
1 head of garlic, unpeeled
2 stems of rosemary, leaves removed
1 large organic chicken, washed and dried
1 cup white wine or chicken stock
Salt

Stuffing
1 large onion, finely chopped

2 cups fresh breadcrumbs
$1/2$ tsp each sage, thyme, parsley
Pinch of nutmeg
Salt and pepper
75g butter

To serve
Bread sauce
Gravy
Steamed vegetables of your choice

1. Preheat the oven to 220°C/ gas mark 7.
2. First make the stuffing. Fry onion in butter until soft. Add the herbs, seasonings and breadcrumbs. Spoon the stuffing into a small greased casserole, cover with buttered foil and cook alongside the chicken.
3. Arrange potatoes and garlic in a large ovenproof dish. Sprinkle with half of the rosemary leaves. Top with the chicken. Pour over the wine or chicken stock. Sprinkle with the remaining rosemary and salt.
4. Cook for an hour and then reduce the oven temperature to 180°C and cook for a further 45 minutes, basting 2 or 3 times. The chicken is cooked when the juices run clear when you pierce the thigh with a sharp knife.
5. Place on a serving platter surrounded by the potatoes and roasted garlic.
6. Serve with the stuffing, gravy, bread sauce and steamed vegetables of your choice.

NUTRIENT ANALYSIS FOR ONE SERVING

Fat	18g	Energy	625kcal	Sodium	.6g
Carbs	77g	Protein	38g	Fibre	6g

Q&A

Favourite restaurant:
Cayenne, Belfast

Favourite sporting hero:
Marvin Magler

Ever played with fear of injury?
No, but I'm always aware of the risk

Party piece:
The Full Monty impersonation

Ever tried the Atkins diet?
No, as you can tell from my figure!

Kevin was educated at South Bristol College. He won his first full cap in November '97 when coming on as a replacement against the All-Blacks and has been a member of the squad ever since. Kevin is now the most capped centre in the history of Irish rugby, leaving him joint second in the all-time caps list. He played in all five games in the RWC 2003 scoring a late individual try in the loss to France. Despite losing his place after defeat in Paris in 2004 he has been ever-present in the squad either starting or as a replacement. He moved to Ulster in the summer of 2004 and one can see his experience spreading throughout a very young and promising Ulster squad

BUTTERMILK PANCAKES WITH BANANAS & MAPLE SYRUP

PRE-MATCH FAVOURITE PRE-MATCH

SERVES 4

375ml milk
125ml buttermilk
225g flour
2tsp sugar
1tsp baking soda
Butter for frying

To serve
2 bananas, sliced
Maple syrup

1. Heat milk and buttermilk gently until hot. Add butter, remove from heat and cool to lukewarm temperature.

2. Sift flour, baking soda and salt into a bowl. Add sugar, fold in the liquid and stir thoroughly to combine.

3. Heat a little butter in a heavy frying pan. Drop spoonfuls of the batter into the frying pan to form small pancakes and cook for 1 minute until bubbles appear. Turn, cook until golden brown, remove and keep warm.

4. Melt a little more butter in the pan and repeat the process until all the batter is used up.

5. To serve, stack the pancakes with bananas in between each layer and drizzle with maple syrup.

NUTRIENT ANALYSIS FOR ONE SERVING

Fat	5g	Energy	286kcal	Sodium	.2g
Carbs	53g	Protein	10g	Fibre	2g

POST-MATCH FAVOURITE POST-MATCH

LASAGNE & CHIPS

SERVES 4

For the filling
2 small onions, peeled and chopped
1 garlic clove, crushed
1tsp olive oil
600g steak mince
1 x 415g tin of chopped tomatoes
4tsp tomato purée
1 small green pepper, seeded
and chopped
1 small red pepper, seeded
and chopped
100g mushrooms, sliced

$^1/_2$ tsp dried oregano
A good pinch of sugar, salt and freshly
ground pepper
400g precooked lasagne sheets

For the sauce
2tbsp plain flour
250ml milk
30g butter
$^1/_4$ tsp nutmeg
100g cheddar cheese, grated
Salt and freshly ground pepper

1. For the filling, sauté the onion and garlic in oil. Add the mince and brown.
2. Add the tomatoes, tomato purée, peppers and mushrooms, oregano, sugar and seasoning to taste. Cover and simmer for 5 to 10 minutes until rich and thick. Remove from the heat.
3. To make the sauce, melt butter, stir in flour and cook, stirring for 1 minute. Gradually stir in the milk. Bring to the boil, then reduce heat and cook, stirring until thick and bubbly. Stir in $^3/_4$ of the cheese and season with nutmeg, salt and pepper. To assemble, layer lasagne sheets with cheese sauce and meat mixture in a baking dish, finishing with cheese sauce. Sprinkle with remaining cheese.
5. Cover and bake at 180°C for 25 minutes. Then bake uncovered for 15 minutes. Remove from the oven and serve with chips.

NUTRIENT ANALYSIS FOR ONE SERVING

Fat	46g	Energy	698kcal	Sodium	.5g
Carbs	29g	Protein	45g	Fibre	2g

Q&A

Favourite restaurant:
The Case in Leicester

Favourite sporting hero:
Muhammad Ali

Party piece:
The Reverse Pothole

3 things I always have in my fridge:
Milk, butter, eggs

If I wasn't a professional rugby player:
I'd be an actor

Geordan was born in Dublin and educated at Newbridge College, Auckland Grammar School and Waterford Institute of Technology. He started his rugby career while at school and in 1997 he was signed up by English club side Leicester Tigers where he has been a regular ever since. He regularly features in the Premiership XV of the season and is one of the most naturally gifted footballers Ireland has ever produced. He has won two Heineken Cups with Leicester scoring a try in their 2002 victory over Munster. In March 2000 he was called into the Ireland squad to win his first cap and went on to win further caps before cruelly breaking his leg in a warm-up match before the RWC 2003. Since then he has been a regular either at wing or full-back. Geordan was named in the 2005 British & Irish Lions squad, and the 27-year-old made the test team for the final game of the series.

JACKET POTATO WITH BAKED BEANS & CHICKEN

PRE-MATCH **FAVOURITE** PRE-MATCH

GEORDAN MURPHY

SERVES 4

4 large baking potatoes
Small amount of oil
1 tin baked beans in tomato sauce
4 cooked chicken fillets, cut into strips
1tbsp olive oil
2tbsp fresh coriander, chopped

To serve
Poached eggs
Hot buttered toast

1. Preheat the oven to 200ºC/gas mark 6.
2. Wash the potatoes well, dry them and prick several times with a fork. Pour some oil into your hands and rub over the potatoes, then scatter over some sea salt.
3. Place the potatoes on to a baking tray and bake in the oven for 1 ¼ – 1 ½ hours. When cooked, the potato should be golden and crispy on the outside and give a little when squeezed. Leave in the oven until needed.
4. Fry the chicken strips and coriander for 2 minutes in the olive oil. Set aside. Heat the beans in a pan.
5. Serve the chicken strips with the beans piled up on top of each baked potato, accompanied by poached eggs and hot buttered toast.

NUTRIENT ANALYSIS FOR ONE SERVING

Fat	8g	Energy	357kcal	Sodium	.2g
Carbs	26g	Protein	46g	Fibre	4g

POST-MATCH FAVOURITE POST-MATCH

CRISPY GRILLED SALMON WITH HORSERADISH SAUCE

SERVES 4

4 salmon cutlets
200ml crème fraiche
1tbsp horseradish sauce
2tbsp fresh white breadcrumbs

To serve
4 baked potatoes
Broccoli and carrots

1. Line a grill rack with foil, brush lightly with oil and cook the salmon under a preheated grill for about 5 minutes on each side, depending on the thickness of the fish fillets, turning once.
2. Meanwhile, combine the crème fraiche and horseradish sauce. Spoon over the salmon and sprinkle with the breadcrumbs.
3. Grill until the topping is golden and crisp.
4. Serve with the baked potatoes, boiled broccoli and carrots.

NUTRIENT ANALYSIS FOR ONE SERVING

| Fat | 32g | Energy | 403kcal | Sodium | .2g |
| Carbs | 8g | Protein | 20g | Fibre | .4g |

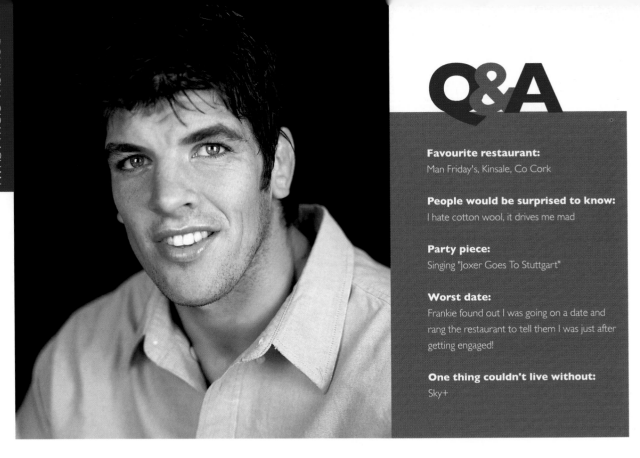

DONNCHA O'CALLAGHAN

Q&A

Favourite restaurant:
Man Friday's, Kinsale, Co Cork

People would be surprised to know:
I hate cotton wool, it drives me mad

Party piece:
Singing "Joxer Goes To Stuttgart"

Worst date:
Frankie found out I was going on a date and rang the restaurant to tell them I was just after getting engaged!

One thing couldn't live without:
Sky+

Donncha was born in Cork and educated at Christian Brothers College. He won international recognition for the first time against England Schools at Lansdowne Road in March 1997 and featured on the Ireland Under-19 side that won the FIRA World Youth Championship. The inevitable first 'A' cap arrived when he came on as a replacement against Scotland in March 2002 and a year later he won his first Senior cap. The Corkman won seven more caps off the bench before winning his place in the starting XV for the Six Nations clash against Wales in February 2004. Coach Eddie O'Sullivan used the Munster giant as a second-half replacement against Italy, Scotland and Wales in last season's Six Nations. He was named in Sir Clive Woodward's British & Irish Lions squad for the 2005 tour to New Zealand, where he played in the final two test matches in the series.

CHICKEN & CORN RISOTTO

DONNCHA O'CALLAGHAN

SERVES 3 - 4

Olive Oil
1 onion, finely chopped
1¹/₂ cups of Arborio rice
400g chicken fillet, cut into strips
425g baby corn spears
1 small red pepper, deseeded and sliced
1 cup frozen peas
750ml chicken stock
¹/₂ cup tomato-based pasta sauce
2tbsp fresh basil & fresh parsley
Black pepper to taste

To serve
Parmesan cheese

1. Heat the olive oil in a heavy-based saucepan. Sauté the onions until pale and translucent, then add the chicken and stir-fry until almost cooked through. Add the rice to the pan and stir until all the grains are coated.
2. Add the corn spears, red pepper, peas and tomato sauce and stir to combine.
3. Add about a ladle full of stock and keep stirring until all the liquid is absorbed. Repeat until all the stock is used up.
4. Stir through the fresh herbs and season to taste. Serve immediately with a sprinkling of parmesan cheese.

NUTRIENT ANALYSIS FOR ONE SERVING

Fat	12g	**Energy**	601kcal	**Sodium**	.6g
Carbs	82g	**Protein**	46g	**Fibre**	8g

DONNCHA O'CALLAGHAN

POST-MATCH **FAVOURITE** POST-MATCH

HOME-MADE BURGERS & OVEN WEDGES

SERVES 4

450g lean organic minced beef
1 large fresh egg, beaten
110g onion, finely chopped
4tbsp tomato ketchup
3tbsp fresh parsley
25g non-salted pistachio nuts, shelled
and chopped
25g brown breadcrumbs
1tsp English mustard

Salt
Worcestershire sauce
Olive oil

To serve
Burger buns
Lettuce
Tomatoes
Oven wedges

1. Place the mince, egg, onion, ketchup, parsley, pistachio nuts, breadcrumbs and mustard in a large bowl and mix to combine. Season to taste with salt and a good dash of Worcestershire sauce.

2. Combine thoroughly and shape into burger patties with wetted hands.

3. Heat olive oil in a heavy-based frying pan and fry patties for about 5 minutes on each side or until cooked through.

4. Toast the burger buns under the grill until golden and assemble burgers by layering the lettuce, patties and tomatoes.

5. Serve with oven wedges.

NUTRIENT ANALYSIS FOR ONE SERVING

Fat	14g	**Energy**	250kcal	**Sodium**	.7g
Carbs	14g	**Protein**	18g	**Fibre**	2g

When it comes to the right recipe for insurance talk to Arachas

ARACHAS

The Irish for Insurance

CORK
9 Eastgate Avenue,
Eastgate Business Park,
Little Island,
Cork.
Phone: 021 427 0505

DUBLIN
The Courtyard,
Carmanhall Road,
Sandyford Industrial Estate,
Dublin 18
Phone: 01 213 5000

Q&A

Favourite restaurant:
Tuscany Bistro, Limerick

If a streaker tried to tackle:
I'd let her if it was a girl and run if it was a man!

American Pie or American Beauty?
American Pie

Italian or Chinese food?
Italian

Favourite sporting hero?
Roy Keane

Paul was educated at Ard Scoil Ris in Limerick and won his first full cap in February 2002 against Wales scoring a try on his debut. Injury forced him to miss the subsequent Six Nations ties against England and Scotland, but he returned to win caps as a replacement against Italy and France, and also played against the All Blacks on the summer tour. After the summer tour of 2003 Paul enjoyed an influential RWC 2003 campaign. Having enjoyed an influential RWC 2003 campaign, he was nominated to lead Ireland in their opening 2004 Six Nations game against France in the absence of the injured Brian O'Driscoll. He skippered the side for a second time in last season's 40-13 win over Scotland, marking the occasion with a first-half try. The 26-year-old was included in the British & Irish Lions squad for last summer's tour to New Zealand, where he played in all three test matches.

PRE-MATCH *FAVOURITE* PRE-MATCH

KEDGEREE

SERVES 4

450g smoked haddock fillets
2 bay leaves
100ml water
120g basmati rice
3 tbsp olive oil
5 spring onions, finely chopped
1 garlic clove, finely chopped
1 tbsp curry powder

Juice of 1 lemon
2 hard-boiled eggs
2 tbsp fresh coriander
Freshly ground black pepper

To serve
Lemon wedges

1. Put the haddock, bay leaves and water in a frying pan and bring to boil. Cover, reduce heat and simmer for 5 minutes. Remove the pan from the heat, drain and when cool enough to handle, remove the skin from the fish and flake the flesh with a fork. Set aside.

2. Meanwhile bring a large saucepan of water to the boil. Add the rice and return to the boil. Stir, then reduce the heat and simmer for 10 minutes until the rice is cooked but still has a slight bite to it. Drain and reserve.

3. Heat a large, non-stick frying pan. Add the oil, spring onions and garlic and fry gently until softened and slightly coloured. Add the curry powder and cook for 2 minutes. Add the lemon juice, the reserved haddock and rice. Cut one egg into wedges and reserve. Chop the other one into small pieces and add to the pan. Sprinkle with the coriander and season to taste with pepper. Continue to heat, stirring gently, until piping hot.

4. Transfer the kedgeree to a warm serving dish. Top with the egg and lemon wedges and serve immediately.

NUTRIENT ANALYSIS FOR ONE SERVING

Fat	16g	Energy	380kcal	Sodium	.4g
Carbs	27g	Protein	33g	Fibre	0g

PAUL O'CONNELL

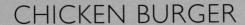

CHICKEN BURGER

SERVES 4

4 chicken breast fillets
4 bread rolls
2tbsp olive oil
Salt & ground pepper to taste
8 butter lettuce leaves, washed and trimmed
2 medium ripe tomatoes, sliced
80ml ($1/3$ cup) mayonnaise

1. Preheat a grill pan or frying pan over medium-high heat.
2. Lightly brush the bread rolls on both sides with $1^1/2$ tbsp of the oil. Place them on the grill pan and cook for 2–3 minutes one each side or until golden. Set aside.
3. Rub the chicken fillets with salt and pepper to taste. Brush the grill pan with the remaining oil and cook the chicken for 5 minutes one each side or until cooked through.
4. Place the bottom halves of the bread rolls onto serving plates, top with lettuce leaves, tomato slices and the chicken. Top with a spoonful of mayonnaise and cover with the bread roll tops.

NUTRIENT ANALYSIS FOR ONE SERVING

Fat	27g	Energy	469kcal	Sodium	.3g
Carbs	17g	Protein	40g	Fibre	1.4g

Q&A

Favourite restaurant:
Da Roberto's, Salthill, Galway

If a streaker tried to tackle me:
It would depend on what she looks like!

Snow Patrol or Franz Ferdinand:
Snow Patrol

Party piece:
Impersonations

Worst date:
Shopping

Johnny was educated at St. Enda's and Garbally College. While at school he won both Junior and Senior Cup medals, and in 1998 he was captain of the Corinthians side that won the Under-19 All-Ireland League. He played for his country five times at that age level and in November 2000 he made his debut for the Ireland Under-25 side when scoring a try in their defeat of Japan at Ravenhill. In February 2001 he made his Ireland 'A' debut against Italy, but unfortunately due to injury, he missed playing in Wasps' Heineken Cup Final victory. Fit again, he was called into the Ireland side to win his first cap in November 2004 against South Africa. Before the month was over he also played against Argentina. Johnny did not play in the opening Six-Nations fixture against Italy but he was ever-present for the remainder of the tournament. He was voted as the BT IRUPA Players' Player of the Year by his peers and became the first player to do so whilst playing outside Ireland. He won his seventh cap during the Ireland summer tour to Japan.

PRE-MATCH **FAVOURITE** PRE-MATCH

PENNE WITH CHICKEN, BACON & TOMATO SAUCE

SERVES 4

500g penne
2tbsp olive oil
1 onion, sliced
2 cloves garlic, crushed
250g chicken fillets, chopped
125g rindless bacon, chopped
1 tin chopped tomatoes
1/2 cup white wine or chicken stock
1/2 cup cream

Salt and freshly ground black pepper to taste

To serve
Basil leaves, torn
Parmesan cheese
Salad
Crusty bread

1. Cook pasta in plenty of boiling salted water until al dente. Drain well and keep warm.
2. Heat oil in a large frying pan and sauté onion and garlic over medium heat until the onion is tender.
3. Add the bacon and chicken and cook until the chicken is cooked through.
4. Add tomatoes and wine or stock. Bring to the boil. Reduce heat and simmer until slightly reduced.
5. Stir in the cream and seasonings. Bring to the boil, reduce heat and simmer until the sauce begins to thicken.
6. Toss through the pasta and heat, stirring for 2 minutes. Serve topped with basil and parmesan. Accompany with salad and crusty bread.

NUTRIENT ANALYSIS FOR ONE SERVING

Fat	19g	Energy	621kcal	Sodium	.6g
Carbs	72g	Protein	42g	Fibre	.2g

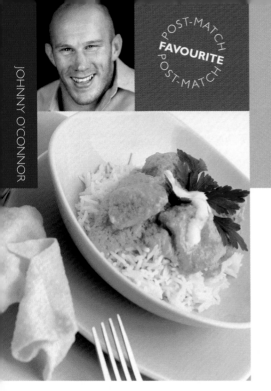

JOHNNY O'CONNOR

POST-MATCH
FAVOURITE
POST-MATCH

CHICKEN KORMA

SERVES 4

2tbsp vegetable oil
375g skinless, boneless chicken breasts, cut into bite-sized pieces
1 onion, sliced
$2^{1}/_{2}$ tbsp korma curry powder
150ml chicken stock
1tsp tomato puree
1tsp caster sugar
75g tomatoes, roughly chopped
150ml cream
25g ground almonds
Salt

To serve
Rice

1. Heat the oil in a saucepan and add the chicken and onion. Fry over gentle heat, stirring occasionally for 6 minutes or until the onion is soft and the chicken is lightly coloured. Stir in the curry powder and cook for a further 2 minutes.
2. Add the stock, tomato purée, sugar, tomatoes, cream and a little salt. Stir to combine the ingredients, bring to the boil, then reduce the heat, cover the pan and simmer gently for 30 minutes, stirring occasionally.
3. Stir the ground almonds into the curry and simmer for 1 minute to thicken the sauce. Taste and adjust seasoning if necessary.
4. Serve the Korma hot with rice.

NUTRIENT ANALYSIS FOR ONE SERVING

Fat	19g	Energy	329kcal	Sodium	.3g
Carbs	7g	Protein	33g	Fibre	1g

Q&A

Favourite restaurant:
Isaac's, McCurtin Street, Cork

Party piece:
"Lady in Red" by Chris De Burgh

People would be surprised to know:
I like to speak French

Favourite place in the world to visit:
Barbados

If I wasn't a professional rugby player:
I'd be a horse trainer

Ronan was born in San Diego, USA and educated in Presentation Cork and UCC. In 1997 he made his Ireland Under-21 debut against Scotland. In 1998 he helped Ireland U21s to win the Triple Crown and won his first 'A' cap against Italy. He won his first Ireland cap against Scotland in the spring of 2000. He scored his first international try in the opening game of the 2001 Six Nations and he then travelled to Australia with the British & Irish Lions playing in two games. He then traded places with David Humphreys for a couple of seasons before cementing himself as Ireland's first choice over the last two seasons. He was selected to tour New Zealand with the Lions, where he won his first Lions cap in the final test match.

PRE-MATCH
FAVOURITE
PRE-MATCH

CHICKEN & PASTA SALAD

SERVES 6

3 cooked chicken breasts, sliced into strips
100g pasta bows, cooked and cooled
100g canned sweetcorn
18 small cherry tomatoes, cut in half
2 spring onions, sliced thinly
$^1/_2$ baby gem lettuce, shredded

Dressing
3tbsp olive oil
1tbsp white wine vinegar
$^1/_2$ tsp sugar
Salt and pepper

To serve
Crusty bread

1. To make the dressing, whisk together all the ingredients in a bowl.
2. Combine all the ingredients for the salad with the chicken and toss in the dressing.
3. Serve the salad in bowls with crusty bread.

NUTRIENT ANALYSIS FOR ONE SERVING

Fat	10g	Energy	261kcal	Sodium	.1g
Carbs	19g	Protein	25g	Fibre	2g

POST-MATCH **FAVOURITE** POST-MATCH

CHICKEN FAJITAS WITH GUACAMOLE

SERVES 4

4 cooked chicken breasts,
cut into pieces

Guacamole
1 ripe avocado
4tbsp lemon juice
1/2 small onion, finely chopped
1 garlic clove, crushed
Pinch of ground cumin
2tbsp coriander

1 tomato, peeled, seeded and chopped
Salt
1 chilli, seeded and chopped (optional)

To serve
1 jar tomato salsa
4 flour tortillas
75g iceberg lettuce, shredded
75g cheddar cheese, grated

1. Prepare the guacamole first. Peel, stone and mash the avocadoes, leaving them slightly chunky.
2. Stir in the lemon juice, onion, garlic, ground cumin, coriander and tomato. Season to taste with salt and more lemon juice if required.
3. Add the chopped chilli if you like it hot. Put into a bowl, cover with clingfilm and refrigerate until needed. It is best served within the hour as it discolours quickly.
4. To assemble, heat the tortillas according to the packet instructions. Then place some of the chicken pieces along the centre of each tortilla, top with some tomato salsa, shredded lettuce, grated cheese, guacamole and roll up.

NUTRIENT ANALYSIS FOR ONE SERVING

Fat	11g	Energy	267kcal	Sodium	.1g
Carbs	2g	Protein	44g	Fibre	.2g

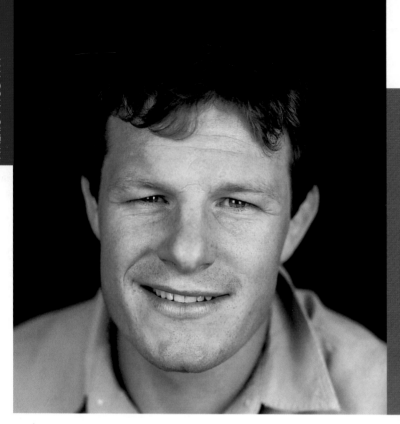

Q&A

Favourite restaurant:
Bijou, Rathgar, Dublin

Party piece:
Flaming limbo

People would be surprised to know:
I was an extra in "Space Truckers" the movie

One thing couldn't live without:
My wife!

If I wasn't a professional rugby player:
I'd be an engineer

Malcolm was born in Essex and educated at Templeogue and Trinity College. Whilst playing with London Irish in November 1997 he was brought into the Ireland Senior side to win his first cap and became a regular fixture in the second row over the next few seasons. He returned from London to Leinster in 1999 and was a member of the WRC 1999 squad. O'Kelly won his 20th cap in February 2000 and scored his first international try against Scotland. He won his 60th cap against France in the 2004 Six Nations opener, and recently became Ireland's most capped player when overtaking centre great Mike Gibson's caps mark of 69. The Leinster forward marked the occasion with a try and a strong season, and was included in Sir Clive Woodward's British & Irish Lions squad's summer tour to New Zealand, but unluckily had to withdraw from the tour due to injury.

CHICKEN DE MAL

SERVES 4

6 chicken breasts, cooked and chopped
300g broccoli
2 cans cream of chicken soup
1 tbsp lemon juice
1 tbsp curry powder
Cheddar cheese (grated)
Breadcrumbs

To serve
Rice

1. Preheat the oven to 200°C.
2. Put a layer of broccoli in the bottom of a rectangular casserole dish.
3. Put layer of chicken over this.
4. Mix the lemon juice and curry powder into the chicken soup and spread on top of chicken.
5. Sprinkle layer of cheese and then bread crumbs over the top.
6. Bake for 30 minutes or until bubbly and serve with rice.

NUTRIENT ANALYSIS FOR ONE SERVING

Fat	11g	Energy	411kcal	Sodium	.5g
Carbs	8g	Protein	69g	Fibre	.2g

POST-MATCH
FAVOURITE
POST-MATCH

SEAFOOD CHOWDER

SERVES 4

Small knob of butter
3 rashers, fried and finely chopped
1 onion, finely chopped
1 fish stock cube dissolved in
1 pint of boiling water
2 medium potatoes, diced
Pint of milk
450g seafood (eg smoked haddock, cod, prawns, mussells)
Pinch of cayenne pepper

To serve
Brown bread

1. Boil potatoes until soft. Remove one half and mash the other half. Set aside.
2. In a deep saucepan, melt the butter and gently fry the onion and bacon.
3. Add the fish stock, potatoes, fish and milk.
4. Stir gently and simmer for 4-5 minutes.
5. Season to taste with a pinch of cayenne pepper.
6. Serve with brown bread.

NUTRIENT ANALYSIS FOR ONE SERVING

| **Fat** | 12g | **Energy** | 291kcal | **Sodium** | .4g |
| **Carbs** | 21g | **Protein** | 27g | **Fibre** | 1.5g |

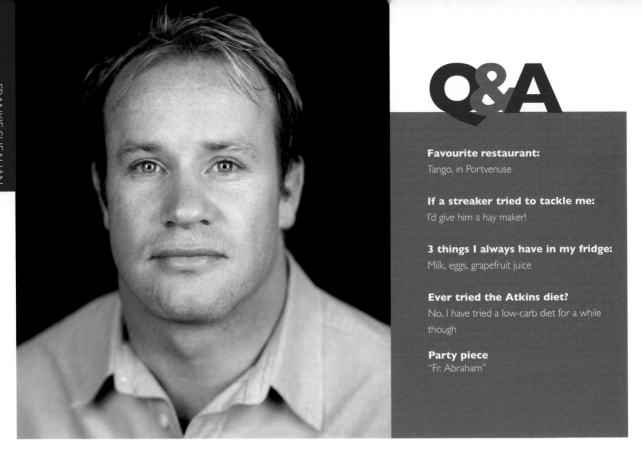

Q&A

Favourite restaurant:
Tango, in Portvenuse

If a streaker tried to tackle me:
I'd give him a hay maker!

3 things I always have in my fridge:
Milk, eggs, grapefruit juice

Ever tried the Atkins diet?
No, I have tried a low-carb diet for a while though

Party piece
"Fr. Abraham"

Frankie was educated at PBC Cork and University College Cork. He won his first cap when coming on as a replacement against the United States during the summer of 2000, and in February 2001 he won his second, again as a replacement against Italy. He started his first international against Romania in June 2001 and again came on against Wales in September of that year. Before the season was over Frankie had scored his first international try when starting against Samoa. He returned to win four caps as a replacement in the 2004 Six Nations and has since added another five caps. Forming part of a talented Munster front-row he has been part of some historic victories with the province and is a strong contender to make the Ireland jersey his own in the coming season. He started both tests against Japan during the 2005 summer tour, scoring three tries over the series.

CHICKEN AND PASTA TWIST BAKE

SERVES 4

FRANKIE SHEAHAN

400g boneless, skinless chicken breasts, cooked and diced
600ml skimmed milk
40g plain flour
Freshly ground black pepper
200g pasta twists
50g fresh wholemeal breadcrumbs

To serve
Green salad

1. Preheat the oven to 190°C/ gas mark 5.
2. Place the milk and flour in a saucepan and bring to the boil over gentle heat, stirring constantly until the sauce thickens. Simmer for 1 minute further, stirring frequently and then season with pepper.
3. Meanwhile cook the pasta in a large pot of salted, boiling water until al dente. Drain immediately.
4. Stir the chicken into the sauce and pour into a 2.4 litre shallow ovenproof dish. Spoon the pasta twists over the sauce, pressing them lightly, without submerging them completely.
5. Sprinkle the breadcrumbs over the top of the pasta and bake for about 20 minutes until the breadcrumbs are golden and crisp.
6. Serve hot with a green salad.

NUTRIENT ANALYSIS FOR ONE SERVING

Fat	4g	Energy	413kcal	Sodium	.2g
Carbs	53g	Protein	45g	Fibre	1g

POST-MATCH **FAVOURITE** POST-MATCH

BEEF IN OYSTER SAUCE

SERVES 4

500g rump steak
2 garlic cloves, crushed
6 spring onions, chopped
3tbsp soy sauce
2tbsp oil
$^1/_3$ cup oyster sauce
1 small red pepper, seeded
and thinly sliced
1 tsp sugar

$^1/_4$ cup white wine
1tsp grated ginger
$^1/_2$ cup beef stock
$^1/_2$ cup mushrooms, sliced
Cornflour

To serve
Steamed rice

1. Cut beef into small, thin slices. Slice onions and mushrooms.
2. Coat meat with a little cornflour and mix with the mushrooms.
3. In a small bowl whisk the beef stock and oyster sauce with 1 tablespoon of cornflour. Transfer to a small saucepan and add the sugar, ginger, soy sauce and wine. Bring to the boil. Simmer for 5 minutes and remove from the heat.
4. In the meantime, heat 2 tablespoons of oil in the bottom of a wok or heavy-based frying pan. Stir-fry the garlic, spring onions and peppers until lightly translucent. Remove from oil and keep warm.
5. Add the meat and mushrooms to the wok and cook for about 1 minute, tossing as it cooks.
6. Return the garlic, green onions and peppers to the meat mixture, top with sauce and stir to combine. Serve immediately with steamed rice.

NUTRIENT ANALYSIS FOR ONE SERVING

| Fat | 13g | Energy | 290kcal | Sodium | .3g |
| Carbs | 11g | Protein | 31g | Fibre | 1g |

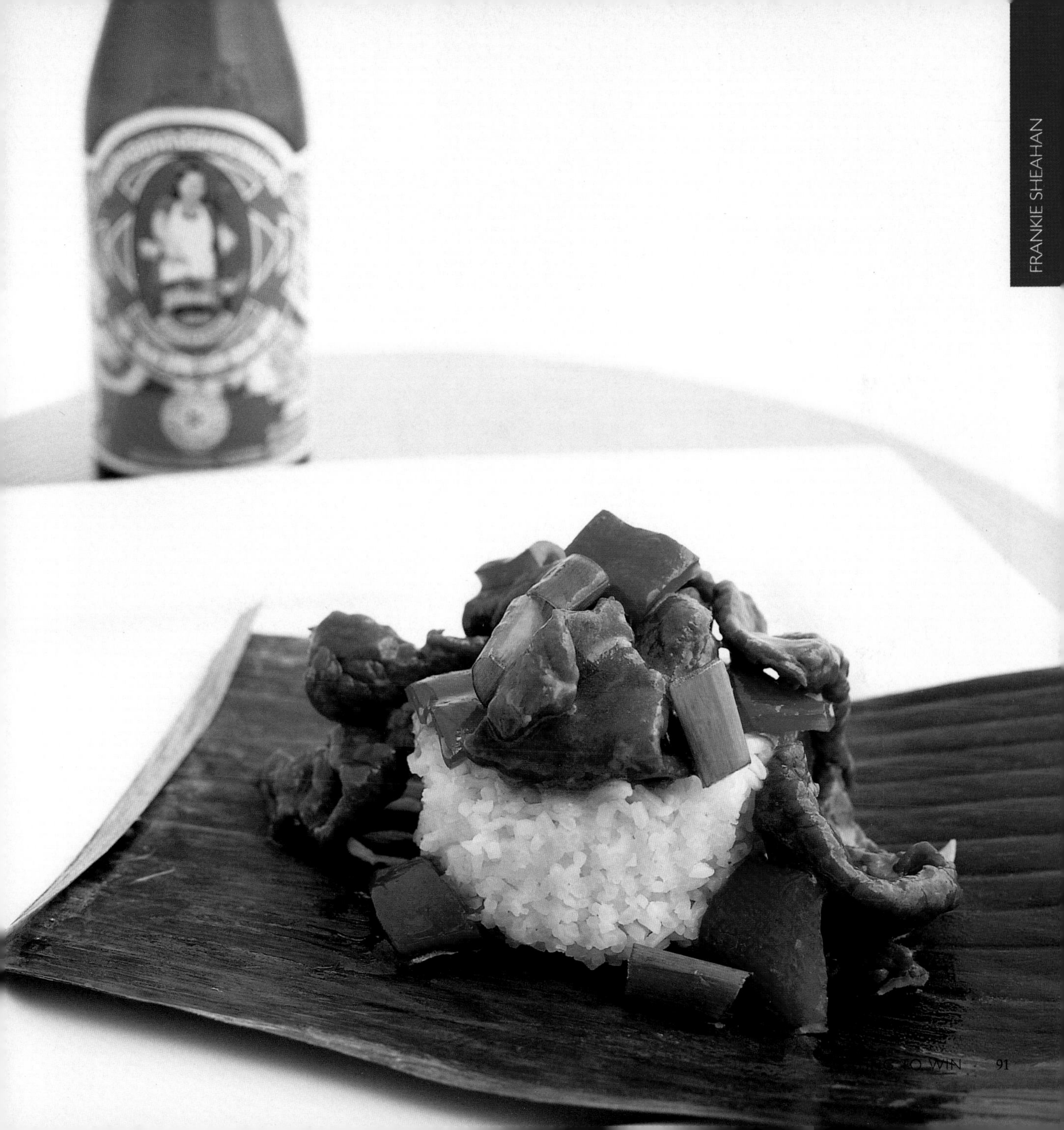

Q&A

Favourite restaurant:
Scoozis, Cork

Favourite sporting hero:
Roy Keane

Italian or Chinese food?
Italian

Party piece:
Not drinking

Worst date:
No complaints so far!

Peter was educated at Presentation Cork and University College Cork. In February 2000 he won his first full cap against Scotland. With the exception of the tour game against the United States in June 2000, he was ever-present in the side until the game against Scotland in September 2001. On that occasion he sat on the replacement bench, although he did win a cap that day when coming on as a replacement for Guy Easterby. He regained his place for the following game against Wales and since then he has enjoyed a tremendous run in the side, only missing four of the last 49 internationals, making him Ireland's most capped scrum-half.

FILLET STEAK WITH PEPPER SAUCE & MASHED POTATOES

PETER STRINGER

SERVES 4

4 fillet steaks
Olive oil
Soy sauce

Mashed potatoes
4 large waxy potatoes
75g butter
$1/4$ cup milk, boiled
Salt and freshly ground pepper

Pepper sauce
$1/4$ cup shallots, finely chopped
2-3 tbsp green or black peppercorns, rinsed
$1/3$ cup dry white wine
$1/3$ cup thick cream
1 tbsp Dijon mustard
$1/2$ tsp dried tarragon
Salt and freshly ground pepper

1. First make the mashed potatoes. Peel and quarter the potatoes and place in a saucepan of cold salted water. Boil until soft, then drain thoroughly. Mash with a vegetable mill and spoon into a saucepan with the butter. Stir thoroughly over a gentle heat and add the boiling milk, beating until it is thick and smooth. Season to taste.
2. Heat a large frying pan and brush with just a slick of oil. Brush each side of the steak lightly with soy sauce and fry quickly, turning once, until done to your liking (3-5 minutes). Salt very lightly and place on a warmed plate.
3. Make the sauce by adding the shallots, peppercorns, wine, cream, mustard, tarragon and seasoning to the pan juices. Bring to the boil and boil rapidly until the sauce is reduced by half. Top the steak with the peppercorn sauce and serve with creamy mashed potatoes.

NUTRIENT ANALYSIS FOR ONE SERVING

Fat	39g	Energy	639kcal	Sodium	.6g
Carbs	33g	Protein	37g	Fibre	3g

POST-MATCH
FAVOURITE
POST-MATCH

PRAWN PHAD THAI

SERVES 4

1 packet (225g) medium rice noodles
Warm water
225g medium-sized prawns, cleaned
1/4 cup nam pla (fish sauce)
1/4 cup and 2tbs sugar
2 cloves garlic, crushed
1/4 cup and 2tbsp white vinegar
1 tsp paprika
Vegetable oil

2 eggs, lightly beaten
1 cup fresh bean sprouts
2 tbsp ground roast chilli

To serve
4 spring onions, slivered
3/4 cup dry roasted peanuts,
finely chopped
Lime wedges

1. *Soak the noodles in warm water for 15 – 20 minutes or until pliable and drain.*
2. *Place bean sprouts in cold water.*
3. *Make the sauce by placing the sugar, vinegar, paprika and nam pla in a bowl and mixing. Set aside.*
4. *Heat a wok and stir-fry the garlic and prawns for a few minutes until cooked through. Add the sauce and stir together.*
5. *Add the noodles and then the eggs by tucking them under the noodles. Add oil as needed. Stir-fry for 2–3 minutes.*
6. *Drain bean sprouts and add to the wok. Stir-fry for another 2–3 minutes.*
7. *Place on a serving dish and garnish with spring onions, peanuts and lime wedges.*

NUTRIENT ANALYSIS FOR ONE SERVING

Fat	5g	Energy	372kcal	Sodium	.4g
Carbs	67g	Protein	18g	Fibre	3g

THE OUT-TAKES
Photos that didn't make the cover

eating to win
RECIPE INDEX

Published on behalf of IRUPA Events Ltd. by:

Zahra Publishing Ltd.
First Floor
19 Railway Road
Dalkey
Co. Dublin
Republic of Ireland

Copyright 2005 IRUPA Events Ltd.
ISBN 0 95 512740 8

To order books contact IRUPA on
+353 1 275 0743 or email
info@irupa.ie

IRUPA Events Limited:
Niall Woods
Publisher:
Gina Miltiadou
Commercial Director:
John Mullins
Editor:
Tara Stevens
Editorial Co-ordinator:
Lorna O'Brien
Consultant Dietitian:
Sarah Keogh
Design and production:
Geoff McGrath
Susan Bell Flavin

Cover and player photography:
Anthony Woods
Food Photography:
Clioné O'Flaherty
Recipe development:
Gina Miltiadou & Emma Parkin
Styling:
Clioné O'Flaherty &
Gina Miltiadou
Special thanks:
Storehouse, Dun Laoghaire for cover
props

All rights reserved. No part of this
publication may be reproduced,
stored in a retrieval system, or